Pat, Pat

Written by Helen Dineen

Collins

Tap it.

Pat it.

pat pat

Sit in a pit.

Sit in a mat.

tip tip

pat pat

7

Sip it.

a tap

Dip in it!

Tim did it!

11

Pat Sam.

Sam

Nap. Nap!

🐾 Review: After reading 🐾

Use your assessment from hearing the children read to choose any GPCs and words that need additional practice.

Read 1: Decoding

- Ask the children to mime the following actions as you read the pages, to check their understanding of the verbs.

  page 2: **Tap**   page 3: **Pat**   page 8: **Sip**   page 13: **Nap**

- Point to **mat** on page 5, allowing the children to sound and blend out loud. Repeat for **Dip** on page 9. Then turn to page 10 and encourage the children to blend in their heads, silently, before reading the words aloud.

- Look at the "I spy sounds" pages (14–15) together. Point to the acrobat and say "acrobat", emphasising the /a/ sound. Ask the children find other things that start with the /a/ sound. (e.g. *ant, astronaut, anchor, apples, ambulance, arrow*). Point to the cat and ask: Where is the /a/ in this word? (*the middle*)

Read 2: Prosody

- Focus on the exclamation marks.

- Turn to page 9, and point to the exclamation mark. Model reading the sentence with feeling. Encourage the children to read page 10 with a feeling such as surprise or annoyance.

- Return to page 10 and talk about what "it" is. Demonstrate how we emphasise the name **Tim** to make it clear who did it! Encourage the children to experiment, emphasising the names **Tim** on page 10, and **Sam** on page 12.

Read 3: Comprehension

- Talk about any cats or dogs the children have met or seen. Which cat or dog do they like best in the book and why?

- Ask the children:

  On page 4, why might a puppy go into a pit? (e.g. *to play*)

  On page 5, why might the cat sit in a mat? (e.g. *to sleep*)

- Encourage the children to talk about other things that cats and dogs really need. (e.g. *to play, kindness, safety, water, food*) Go through the book, identifying how each pet is getting what it needs.